Anonymous

Stowe

A description of the magnificent house and gardens of the Right

Honourable Richard Grenville Temple

Anonymous

Stowe
*A description of the magnificent house and gardens of the Right Honourable
Richard Grenville Temple*

ISBN/EAN: 9783337131319

Printed in Europe, USA, Canada, Australia, Japan

Cover: Foto ©Andreas Hilbeck / pixelio.de

More available books at **www.hansebooks.com**

A

DESCRIPTION

Of the Magnificent

HOUSE and GARDENS

Of the Right Honourable

Richard Grenville Temple,

Earl TEMPLE,

Viscount and Baron *COBHAM*,

One of his MAJESTY's Moft Honourable Privy Council, and
Knight of the moft Noble Order of the Garter.

Embellifhed with a General PLAN of the GARDENS,
and alfo a feparate PLAN of each BUILDING, with
PERSPECTIVE VIEWS of the fame.

A NEW EDITION,

With all the Alterations and Improvements that have been
made therein, to the prefent Time.

With the Defcription of the Infide of the Houfe.

Where Order in Variety we fee,
And where, tho' all Things differ, all agree.—
Nature fhall join you, Time fhall make it grow,
A Work to wonder at—perhaps a STOWE.   POPE.

LONDON:

Printed for J. and F. RIVINGTON in St. *Paul's Church yard*;
B. SEELEY in *Buckingham*, and T. HODGKINSON
at the *New Inn* at *Stowe*. 1769.

*The Defcription of the Houfe and Gardens, without the Plans and Views
of the Temples, may be had alone; Price Six-pence.*

A LIST of the PRINTS,

Drawn in Perspective by SEELEY.

A PLAN of Earl TEMPLE's House and Gardens.

The Corinthian Arch.
One of the Pavilions at the Entrance.
The Shepherd's Cove.
An artificial Piece of Ruins.
The Temple dedicated to Venus.
One of the Lodges.
One of the Pavilions at the Entrance to the Park.
An Egyptian Pyramid.
St. Augustine's Cave.
The Temple of Bacchus.
Nelson's Seat.
The South Front of the House.
Dido's Cave.
The Rotundo
King George II. ⎱ on Columns.
Queen Caroline, ⎰
A Gate-way, by Kent.
A Doric Arch.
A Ruin.
The Temple of ancient Virtue.

The Shell Bridge.
The Temple of British Worthies.
A Gate-way by Leoni.
The Cold Bath.
The Grotto.
The Temple of Concord and Victory.
Capt. Grenville's Monument.
The Lady's Temple.
The Fane of Pastoral Poetry.
The Castle.
An Obelisk to the Memory of General Wolfe.
Lord Cobham's Pillar.
The Gothic Temple.
The Palladian Bridge.
The Temple of Friendship.
The Pebble Alcove.
Congreve's Monument.
An Equestrian Statue of Geo. I.

Also a PLAN of the principal Floor of the House, and PLANS of the Buildings in the Gardens.——All accurately drawn by Mr. Fairchild, Surveyor and Architect.

	s.	d.
The Description of the House and Gardens without the Plans and Views of the Temples, Price	0	6
Ditto——with the Plan of the Gardens ——	1	0
Ditto——with all the Plans and Views stitch'd in blue Paper —— —— ——	3	0
Ditto——half bound —— ——	3	6
Ditto——bound —— ——	4	0
Ditto——gilt and lettered —— ——	5	0

The RIGHT HONOURABLE

The EARL TEMPLE:

This DESCRIPTION

Of his LORDSHIP's

HOUSE and GARDENS

AT

S   T   O   W   E,

Is moſt humbly Dedicated, by his LORDSHIP's

Obliged and moſt obedient

humble Servant,

To the EARL TEMPLE,

On GARDENING.

BY Commerce, *Albion*, and by Arms refin'd,
    Sought for the Charms of Art and Nature join'd;
Along the Banks of her own *Thames* she stray'd,
Where the gay Sisters of the Waters play'd;
In many a soft Meander wildly rov'd,
And grac'd the Meadows which their Stream improv'd.
She mark'd romantic *Windsor*'s warlike Pride,
To Learning's peaceful Seat so nearly ally'd;
Where *Temple*'s Bosom early sigh'd for Praise,
Struck with th' inspiring Fame of ancient Days;
She came where Silver *Thames* and *Isis* bright,
Their friendly Treasures in one Stream unite;
Where Princes, Prelates, fir'd with Patriot Views,
By generous Gifts invited every Muse;
Where every Muse her grateful Tribute brought,
And Virtue practis'd what sound Learning taught;
At length her longing Eyes and hallow'd Feet,
Reach'd verdant STOWE's magnificent Retreat,
Where Fame and Truth had promis'd she should find
Scenes to improve and please her curious Mind.
Each Step Invention, Elegance display'd,
Such, as when *Churchill* woes the *Aonian* Maid,
And joins in easy graceful Negligence,
Th' harmonious Pow'rs of Verse, with *Sterling* Sense;
Such, as when *Poussin*'s or *Albano*'s Hand
On glowing Canvas the rich Landschape plann'd,
And classic Genius strove, by mimic Art,
Thro' the admiring Eye to reach the Heart.
Amidst the Wonders of each striking Scene,
High on the Summit of a sloping Green

A solemn

A folemn Temple, in Proportion true,
Magnificently fimple, courts the View;
Concord and *Victory* with Pride proclaim
This Manfion facred to *Britannia*'s Fame,
Whofe Form * majeftic, from all Hands receives
The various Product ev'ry Region gives,
Pleas'd at her Feet their choiceft Gifts to lay,
And Homage to her Pow'r fuperior pay;
The fculptur'd Walls her Glories paft declare,
In proud Memorials † of fuccefsful War.
No factious Sacrifice to *France* and *Spain*
Thefe confecrated Trophies can profane;
For public ‡ Liberty her awful Seat
Here fixing, here protects her laft Retreat;
Where to the Great and Good in every Shade,
The fragrant Tribute of juft Praife is paid:
Where the prime Beauties form'd by Nature's Hand
Throughout her Works in every diftant Land,
Tranfplanted, flourifh in their native Eafe,
And, as by magic Charm collected, pleafe——
Here the fair Queen of this heroic Ifle
Imperial *Albion*, with a gracious Smile
Confefs'd fhe lovely Nature faw at laft
Unite with Art, and both improve by Tafte.

* The Alto Relievo in the Pediment.
† The Medallions of the Victories.
‡ The Statue of public Liberty placed in the middle Niche of
the Temple.

A

DESCRIPTION

OF THE

GARDENS.

IN the Road from *London* to *Stowe* are the Towns of *Uxbridge, Chalfont, Amersham, Great Miſſenden, Wendover, Ailſbury, Winſlow,* and *Buckingham,* which laſt is diſtant from *London* 57, from *Oxford* 26 Miles.—Here are four capital Inns, the *Cobham Arms,* the *Croſs Keys,* the *George,* and *White Hart* ; a Gravel Road leads to the *New Inn* at *Stowe,* diſtant from *Buckingham* about a Mile and a half, where are good Accommodations : On the left Hand a large *Corinthian* Arch or Gate-way preſents itſelf, from whence appears the Garden Front of his Lordſhip's Houſe, proudly ſtanding on the Summit of a verdant Hill, and encompaſſed by the Garden and Park.——From the *New Inn* you deſcend to the Garden Entrance ; but the Road to the Houſe leads by, or through the *Corinthian* Arch, and is beautifully diverſified with Hill, Valley, Lawn, River, and a perpetual Change of Scene ariſing from the numerous Buildings intermixt with Wood, and " boſom'd high in tufted " Trees," which ſtrike the Eye with a moſt pictureſque and ever-varying Magnificence.

At the South Entrance of the Gardens are two Pavilions fupported by *Doric* Pillars.

Here you have a View, very ftriking at firft Entrance, of the Houfe; the two Rivers on the Right-hand meeting in one Stream, run into a Kind of Bay, (which was formerly an Octagon, and in the Centre ftood an Obelifk, now removed into the Park.) The beautiful Difpofition of the Lawns, Trees, and Buildings at a Diftance, gives us a Kind of Earneft of what our Expectation is raifed to

Turning to the Left-hand you defcend to

An artificial Piece of Ruins, of a Temple of two River-Gods,

Covered with Evergreens, and adorned with the Statues of Fauns, Satyrs, and River-Gods; a beautiful Cafcade of three Sheets of Water falls from a River above into a large Lake of ten Acres.

The Shepherd's Cove : Defigned by Mr. *Kent*,

is feated in a rifing Wood, on the Banks of the Lake.

The Temple dedicated to VENUS,

With this Infcription,

VENERI HORTENSI.

It is a fquare Building with circular Arches and Wings, defigned by Mr. *Kent*; the Infide adorned with Paintings by Mr. *Sieter*, taken from *Spenfer*'s *Fairy Queen*.—The Lady is the fair *Hellinore*, who having left a difagreeable Hufband, and wandering in the Woods, was met by the polite Set of Gentry fhe is dancing with : She likes their Manner of Life, and refolves to enjoy it with them. Her old Spoufe *Malbecco* is inconfolable for his Lofs; he wanders many Days in Search of her, and at length finds her (you fee him at a Diftance peeping from behind a Tree) revelling with a beaftly Herd of Satyrs. When the Evening comes on, he follows the Company to their Retirement, takes a commodious Stand, and to his great Torment fees every Thing that paffes among them. After they were all laid afleep, he creeps gently

to

to his Lady, and you fee him in the other Painting offering to be reconciled to her again, if fhe will return back with him. But *Hellinore* threatens to awake the Satyrs, and get him feverely handled if he does not immediately leave her. Upon which the poor ufelefs old Man is obliged to fly, and foon after runs diftracted.—See Book III. of the *Fairy Queen*, Canto 10. The Roof is adorned with a naked *Venus*. Upon the Frize is the following Motto from *Catullus*:

Nunc ame qui nondum amavit ;
Quique amavit, nunc amet.

Let him love now, who never lov'd before :
Let him who always lov'd, now love the more,

The late Q u e e n's Statue

is erected on four *Ionic* Columns.——On the Pedeftal is this Infcription :

D I V Æ C A R O L I N Æ,

To the Divine C A R O L I N E.

Two Pavilions.

One of them is made Ufe of as a Dwelling Houfe ; the other ftands in the Garden ; the Space between forms a grand Gate-way, defigned by *Kent*, which is the Entrance into the Park——From hence there is a noble View of a Bridge, with a fine Serpentine River, and a Road, terminated by two Lodges, which form a grand Approach to the Park and Houfe.

An *Egyptian* Pyramid,

is fixty Feet high. On the Outfide is this Infcription.

Inter plurima hortorum horunce ædificia a Johanne Vanbrugh, *equite, defignata, hanc pyramidem illius memoriæ facram effe voluit* Cobham.

To the Memory of Sir *John Vanbrugh*, by whom feveral of the Buildings in thefe Gardens were defigned, Lord *Cobham* hath erected this Pyramid.

And

And in the Infide,

Lufifti fatis, edifti fatis, atque bibifti,
Tempus abire tibi eft ; ne potum largius æquo
Rideat & pulfet lafciva decentius ætas.

With Pleafure furfeited, advanc'd in Age,
Retire in Time from Life's fantaftic Stage :
Left Youth the great Indecency contemn,
And hifs thee from a Scene defign'd for them.

Linquenda tellus, & domus & placens
Uxor ; neque harum, quas colis, arborum
    Te, præter invifas cupreffos,
      Ulla brevem dominum fequetur.

Thy lofty Palace, thy engaging Wife,
Thy wide Domain, and all the Pride of Life,
Short liv'd, thou foon muft quit, nor thro' the Grove
Rais'd by thy Hand, and cherifh'd by thy Love,
Save the funereal Cyprefs, will a Tree
Be found, in thy laft Hour, to follow Thee.

St. Augustine's Cave,

is a Cell formed of Mofs and Roots of Trees inter-
woven ; this is fituated in a retired Thicket, and
very artfully contrived, in the fame Manner as Shades
in a Picture, or Paufes in Mufic.

   In this Cave is a Straw Couch, a wooden Chair,
three Windows or Holes, over which are three Infcriptions in Monkifh *Latin* Verfe.

On the Right-hand.

Sanctus Pater Auguftinus,
(Prout aliquis divinus
Narrat) contra fenfualem
Actum Veneris lethalem
(Audiat clericus) ex nive
Similem puellam vivæ
Arte mirâ conformabat,
Qua cum bonus vir cubabat

Quod

Quod si fas est in errorem
Tantum cadere doctorem ;
Quæri potest ; an carnalis
Mulier, potius quam nivalis,
Non sit apta ad domandum,
Subigendum, debellandum
Carnis tumidum furorem.
Et importunum ardorem ?
Nam ignis igni pellitur,
Vetus ut verbum loquitur.
Sed, inuptus hac in lite
Appellabo te, marite.

St. *Augustine,* holy Father,
(As from some Divines we gather)
Against the Sin of lewd Embrace,
And Act venereal, his Grace
To fortify (Divines, give Ear,
The pious Precedent revere)
With wond'rous Art a Girl of Snow
Did make, the Life resembling so, }
That th'one from t'other scarce you'd know.
This done, the good Man Side by Side
Lay down t' enjoy his new-form'd Bride.
But if a learned Doctor can
Fall, as might any other Man;
It may be ask'd, with Reason good,
Whether a Girl of Flesh and Blood,
More certain far than one of Snow,
Would not controul, subdue, o'erthrow, }
The swelling, Rebel-flesh below ;
Of Passion cool the Rage and Boiling,
And hinder Nature from recoiling ?
For Fire and Fire, two mortal Foes,
Expel themselves, the Proverb goes,
But I, unmarried, for Decree,
O married Man, appeal to thee.

On

On the Left.

Apparuit mihi, nuper in somnio cum nudis & anhelan-
tibus molliter Papillis & hianti suaviter vultu—Eheu!
benedicite!

Cur gaudes, Satana, muliebrem sumere formam?
Non facies voti casti me rumpere normam.
Heus fugite in cellam; pulchram vitate puellam;
Nam radix mortis fuit olim fæmina in hortis.
Vis fieri fortis? Noli concumbere scortis.
        In sanctum Originem Eunuchum.
Filius Ecclesiæ Origines fortasse probetur:
Esse patrem nunquam se sine teste probet.
        Virtus diaboli est in lumbis.

Satan, why, deck'd in female Charms,
    Doft thou attack my Heart?
My Vow is Proof againft thy Arms,
    'Gainft all thy Wiles and Art.
Ah! Hermits, flee into your Cells,
    Nor Beauty's Poifon feed on,
—The Root of Death (as Story tells)
    Was Woman firft in *Eden*.
Would'ft thou thyfelf a dauntlefs Hero prove,
Deteft th' Enjoyments vile of lawlefs Love.
That *Origen's* true Son of Church, agreed,
But could not for a Father be decreed.
In what we call the Loins, they fay,
The Devil bears the greateft Sway.

Fronting the Door.

Mente pie elatâ, peragro dum dulcia prata,
    Dormiit absque dolo pulchra puella solo;
Multa ostendebat, dum semisupina jacebat,
    Pulchrum os, divinum pectus, aperta sinum.
Ut vidi mammas, concepi extempore flammas,
    Et dicturus ave dico, Maria, cave:
Nam magno totus violenter turbine motus
    Pœne illam invado, pœne & in ora cado.

Illa sed haud lentè surgit, curritque repentè,
  Currit &, invito me, fugit illa citò,
Fugit causa mali tamen effectus satanali,
  Internoque meum cor vorat igne reum;
O inferne canis, cur quotidie est tibi panis,
  Per visus miros sollicitare viros?
Cur monachos velles fieri tam carne rebelles,
  Nec castæ legi turbida membra regi?
Jam tibi jam bellum dico, jam triste flagellum
  Esuriemque paro, queis subigenda caro.
Quin abscindatur, ne pars sincera trahatur,
  Radix, quâ solus nascitur usque dolus.

As lost in Thought, and Contemplation deep,
I wander o'er the verdant Meads—in Sleep;
Sleep undesigning, lo! repos'd a Maid,
Fresh as the Verdure of her grassy Bed,
Reclin'd in Posture half supine she lay,
A World of Beauties did her Form display:
Her Face, her Neck divine, her Bosom too,
With all their Charms were open to my View.
Her heaving Globes no sooner struck my Eye,
But strait the Flames thro' all my Vitals fly.
I would have said my *Ave-Mary-Pray'r*,
But, stead of that, I cry'd out, *Maid beware.*
For in the Whirlwind of strong Passion tost,
And Reason in the vi'lent Transport lost
I almost seize the fair, inviting Prey,
And to her Lips impatient urge my Way;
She sudden starts, and with a rapid Flight,
Shoots from my Touch, and leaves my ravish'd Sight.
The Cause of Evil's fled—th' Effect remains,
And still too furious revels in my Veins:
Has kindled an infernal, fatal Flame,
Which inward burns thro' all my guilty Frame.
Why is't thy daily Food, O hellish Cur!
Man up to Vice by wond'rous Sights to spur?
Why is't thy Pleasure, *Monks* should thus rebel,
Their fleshly Members 'gainst their Laws should swell?
'Gainst

'Gainſt thee I now eternal War declare,
The Laſh ſevere, and Hunger I prepare ;
With theſe to mortify my carnal Luſt,
To theſe my Virtue, Chaſtity to truſt.
But leſt the Part that's whole, ſhould be infected,
That Modeſty may better be protected,
Beſt, once for all, to cut away the Root,
From whence alone our guilty Paſſions ſhoot.

Near this holy Father's Cell, upon a Stone, is
engraved the following monumental Inſcription.

To the Memory
of
SIGNIOR FIDO,
an *Italian* of good Extraction ;
who came into *England*,
not to bite us, like moſt of his Countrymen,
but to gain an honeſt Livelihood.
He hunted not after Fame,
yet acquired it ;
regardleſs of the Praiſe of his Friends,
but moſt ſenſible of their Love.
Tho' he liv'd amongſt the Great,
he neither learn'd nor flatter'd any Vice.
He was no Bigot,
Tho' he doubted of none of the 39 Articles.
And, if to follow Nature,
and to reſpect the Laws of Society,
be Philoſophy,
he was a perfect Philoſopher ;
a faithful Friend,
an agreeable Companion,
a loving Huſband,
diſtinguſh'd by a numerous Offspring,
all which he lived to ſee take good Courſes.
In his old Age he retir'd
to the Houſe of a Clergyman in the Country,
where he finiſh'd his earthly Race,
And died an Honour and an Example to the whole Species.

Reader,

Reader,

This Stone is guiltlefs of Flattery,
for he to whom it is infcrib'd
was not a Man,
but a
Grey-hound.

The Temple of BACCHUS

is a ftucco'd Building; the Infide adorned with the Revels of *Bacchus*, painted by *Nollikins*.————This Building commands a great Part of the Gardens, and a beautiful Profpect over the Country.

NELSON's Seat

is an airy Building of Sir *John Vanbrugh*'s to the North-weft of the Houfe, from whence there is an open Profpect; and in it are the following Infcriptions, defcribing the Paintings.

On the Right Hand.

Ultra Euphratem & Tigrim
ufque ad oceanum propagatâ ditione
Orbis terrarum imperium Romæ adfignat optimus princeps,
cui fuper advolat Victoria
laurigerum fertum hinc inde
utraque manu extendens
comitantibus Pietate & Abundantiâ.
In arcu Conftantini.

Having extended his Power beyond the *Euphrates* and *Tigris,*
as far as the Ocean,
this moft potent Prince
affigns the Empire of the World to *Rome:*
over whom Victory flies,
waving a Laurel Crown,
accompanied with *Piety* and *Plenty.*
Upon *Conftantine*'s Arch.

On

On the Left.

Poſt obitum L. Veri,
in imperio cùm Marco conſortis,
Roma
integram orbis terrarum
poteſtatem ei & in eo contulit.

In Capitolio.

After the Death of *Lucius Verus*
Partner in the Empire with *Marcus,*
Rome
conferred on him
the Empire of the World.

In the Capitol.

Oppoſite the North Front of the Houſe, at the Head of the Canal, is the Equeſtrian Statue of King *George* I. in Armour with this Inſcription:

In medio mihi Cæſar erit,
Et viridi in campo ſignum de marmore ponam.

COBHAM.

Imperial *Cæſar*'s Statue I will place,
Full in the Centre on the verdant Graſs.

To this Front there is a Wall ornamented with Niches, and two Gate-ways into the Courts, by *Kent;* two Gate-ways into the Gardens, by *Leoni.*

Oppoſite the South Front is a grand Parterre, where you have a diſtant View of many beautiful Objects in the Garden, and a fine Proſpect over the Country.

The Statue of his late Majeſty,
erected on a *Corinthian* Pillar, with this Inſcription :

GEORGIO AUGUSTO.

On her Royal Highneſs the Princeſs AMELIA's Arrival at STOWE.

Apollo * and his tuneful Maids,
Who range their lov'd *Aonian* Glades,

* Statue of *Apollo* and the *Muſes.*

Forſook

Forfook the *Heliconian* Spring,
To hail the Daughter of a King.
Fond *Echo* fhew'd them where to try,
The fweeteft Pow'rs of Melody.
Clofe by the Image of her Sire,
Apollo touch'd the founding Lyre.
I faw the aweful Statue * fmile,
The Guardian of this happy Ifle,
When regal State with Freedom ftrove,
Which moft fhould gain the others Love!
Mild he furvey'd the pleafing Scene,
And thus addrefs' his much-lov'd Queen,
Whofe fculptur'd † Form majeftic ftood,
The Glory of the neighbouring Wood ;
Soft Partner of my happieft Days,
Grac'd with a grateful People's Praife,
The joyful Hour approaches near,
Which brings our fav'rite Daughter here.
She will revere the hallow'd Ground,
Where ancient ‡ Virtue's Dome is found,
And view the Shrine with Heart-felt Pride,
Where *Englifh* Worthies ftill prefide ;
Where every Virtue ftands confeft,
Juft Emblem of her generous Breaft.
Nor will her Recollection fail,
In Victory's ‖ confecrated Vale,
To glory in the *Brunfwick* Name,
For there the Trophies § of my Fame
Remain unfullied yet.—The reft
A Sigh and rifing Tear fupprefs'd.
Apollo footh'd the mournful King ;
He tun'd to Joy the golden String ;
Then fung of Royal *Emily*,
When Light'ning darts from either Eye,

* Statue of King *George* II.
† The Statue of Queen *Caroline*.
‡ The Temple of *Ancient Virtue.*
‖ The Temple of *Concord* and *Victory.*
§ Medallions of the Victories gained in the late War, placed round the Temple.

And

And Spirit in her meaning Face
Adds Dignity and Senfe to Grace ;
Or, when Compaffion melts her Mind,
In Tendernefs to human Kind,
And her rich Bounty copious flows,
In Streams as various as their Woes ;
Or, when amidft the circling Great,
She graceful moves in royal State,
Difpenfing round with Judgment true,
Honour to all where Honour's due :
Or, when fhe condefcends to ftand,
The firft in Friendfhip's fpotlefs Band,
Preferring to the Courtiers Art
Truth and Simplicity of Heart !
In Air th' inchanting Mufic floats ;
The Zephyrs catch the varied Notes,
And bear to Heav'n th' enraptur'd Lays,
Fraught with *Amelia*'s flowing Praife.
The Mother heard th' applauding Choir,
Her Breaft extatic Tranfports fire ;
As on the Day her martial Son,
Culloden's glorious Triumph won.
When lo ! upon the flow'ry Green
Her darling *Emily* is feen ;
What Hand can paint the glowing Cheek,
The beating Heart, the Looks that fpeak ?
What but *Apollo*'s Lyre exprefs
The full maternal Tendernefs.
Thus flufh'd with Pride and ardent Love
Latona views her Twins from *Jove*,
Confcious, fhe on the *Delian* Earth
To two Divinities gave Birth.

DIDO's Cave,

with this Infcription :

Speluncum Dido, dux & Trojanus, eandem
Deveniunt—— VIRG.

  ⸰ Repairing to the fame dark Cave are feen,
    The *Trojan* Hero and the *Tyrian* Queen.

E 3 A   The

The ROTUNDO

is raifed upon *Ionic* Pillars, and is ornamented with a Statue of the *Venus* of *Medicis.*—The Building by Sir *John Vanburgh*, altered by *Borra*.

From hence you pafs into the great Avenue, where on the Right-hand, you have the Profpect of the *Corinthian* Gate-way, and Entrance to the Gardens (mentioned before); and on the Left, the Houfe, near which

A Doric Arch,

ftanding on an Eminence, and accompanied with the Statues of *Apollo* and the nine *Mufes*, forms an Entrance into a very pleafing Scene.

On the Back Front of the *Attic* is infcribed

AMELIÆ SOPHIÆ AUG.

To her Royal Highnefs the Princefs *Amelia Sophia.*

Through the Arch is feen the *Palladian* Bridge, and a Caftle on the oppofite Hill, which form a delightful Perfpective.

On the Infide Front of the *Attic* there is a Medallion of H. R H. with this Exergue from *Horace*,

O colenda femper & culta!

O Thou worthy of every Honour, and ever honoured!

VERSES prefented to her Royal Highnefs at her firft Entrance in 1768.

See the bright God adorn'd with all his Rays,
From Heav'n defcends to fing *Amelia*'s Praife:
Their golden Lyres he bids the Sifters bring,
Join the glad Song, and ftrike the founding String:
The deep-ton'd Chord obeys his fkilful Hand,
And all is Harmony where you command.

Under an old Elm, not far diftant, the *Heliconian* Spring is feen to rife.

A Ruin.

The

The Temple of Ancient Virtue,

in a very flourishing Condition ; the Building is a Rotundo of the *Ionic* Order by Mr. *Kent* ; on the Outside, over each Door, is this Motto :

Priscæ Virtuti.

To Ancient Virtue.

And in four Niches within, standing at full Length, are the Statues of *Lycurgus*, *Socrates*, *Homer*, and *Epaminondas* : Under which are the following Inscriptions :

Under LYCURGUS.

Qui summo cum consilio, inventis legibus,
Omnemque contra corruptelam munitis optime,
Pater Patriæ
Libertatem firmissimam
Et mores sanctissimos,
Expulsa cum divitiis avaritiâ, luxuriâ, libidine,
In multa secula.
Civibus suis instituit.

Who having planned, with consummate Wisdom, a System of Laws firmly secured against every Incroachment of Corruption, and having by the Expulsion of Riches, banished Luxury, Avarice, and Intemperance, established in the State for many Ages, perfect Liberty and inviolable Purity of Manners—The Father of his Country.

Under SOCRATES.

Qui corruptissima in civitate innocens,
Bonorum hortator, unici cultor DEI,
Ab inutili otio, & vanis disputationibus,
Ad officia vitæ, & societatis commoda
Philosophiam avocavit,
Hominum sapientissimus.

Who

Who innocent in the Midſt of a moſt corrupted People, the Encourager of the Good, a Worſhipper of the one God, recalled Philoſophy from uſeleſs Speculations and vain Diſputes, to the Duties of Life and the Benefit of Society.—The wiſeſt of Men!

Under HOMER,

Qui poetarum princeps, idem & maximus,
Virtutis præco, & immortalitatis largitor,
Divino carmine
Ad pulchre audendum, & patiendum fortiter,
Omnibus notus gentibus, omnes incitat.

The firſt and the greateſt of the Poets, The Herald of Virtue, The Giver of Immortality; who by his divine Genius, known to all Nations, incites all, nobly to dare, and to ſuffer firmly.

Under EPAMINONDAS.

Cujus a virtute, prudentia, verecundia,
Thebanorum reſpublica
Libertatem ſimul & imperium,
Diſciplinam bellicam, civilem & domeſticam
Accepit ;
Eoque amiſſo, perdidit.

By whoſe Valour, Prudence, Modeſty, the *Theban* Commonwealth gained Liberty and Empire, Military Diſcipline, Civil and Domeſtic Policy, all which, by loſing him, ſhe loſt.

Over one Door.

Charum eſſe civem, bene de republica mereri, laudari,
coli, diligi, glorioſum eſt : metui vero, & in odio eſſe in-
vidioſum, deteſtabile, imbecillum, caducum.

To

To be dear to our Country, to deferve well of the Public, to be honoured, reverenced, loved, is glorious ; but to be dreaded and hated is odious, deteftable, weak, ruinous.

Over the other.

Juſtitiam cole & pietatem, quæ cum ſit magna in parentibus & propinquis, tum in patria maxima eſt. Ea vita via eſt in cælum, & in hunc cœtum eorum qui jam vixerunt.

Cultivate Juftice and Benevolence, which in an eminent Manner is due to Relations and to Friends, but in the higheft Degree to our Country ; this Path leads to the Manfions of the Bleffed, and to the *Affembly* of thofe who are now no more.

From the Doors of this Temple, and from the Periftilium, the Views are charming : From one Door you fee the Statue of the late Queen, and the Caftle, being a Farm-Houfe, ftanding at the End of a Line in the Park three Miles long : From the other Door you fee the Temple of *Britiſh* Worthies, and the *Palladian* Bridge at a Diftance ; as alfo

Captain GRENVILLE's Monument;

being a Naval Column erected by the late Lord *Cobham* in honour of Captain *Grenville*, upon the Top of which Heroic Poetry, fuppofed to light, holds in her Hand a Scroll with

Non niſi Grandia Canto.

Heroic Deeds alone my Theme.

Upon the Plinth and on the Pedeftal are the following Infcriptions :

DIGNUM LAVDE VIRVM MVSA VETAT MORI.

The Mufe forbids Heroic Worth to die.

Sororis

Sororis fuæ Filio,
Thomæ Grenville,
Qui navis præfectus regiæ,
Ducente claffem Britannicam Georgio Anfon,
Dum contra Gallos fortiffimè pugnaret,
Dilaceratæ navis ingenti fragmine,
Femore graviter percuffo,
Perire, dixit moribundus, omnino fatius effe,
Quam inertiæ reum in judicio fifti ;
Columnam hanc roftratam
Laudans & mœrens pofuit
Cobham.
Infigne virtutis, eheu ! rariffimæ
Exemplum habes ;
Ex quo difcas
Quid virum præfectura militari ornatum
Deceat.
M DCC XLVII.

To his Nephew
Thomas Grenville,
Who
Captain of a Ship of War,
In the *Britiſh* Fleet,
Commanded by Admiral *Anfon*,
In an Engagement with the *French*,
Being wounded mortally in the Thigh,
By a Fragment of his ſhatter'd Ship,
Expiring, faid,
" How much better is it thus to die
" Than to ftand arraigned
" Before a Court Martial."
This Naval Column
was erected
By *Richard* Vifcount *Cobham* ;
As a Monument of his Applaufe and Grief,
1747.

From

From this animating Example
Learn
When honour'd with Command,
What becomes
An Officer.

Ye weeping Mufes, Graces, Virtues, tell,
If fince your all-accomplifh'd *Sidney* fell,
You, or afflicted *Britain*, e'er deplor'd
A Lofs like that thefe plaintive Lays record;
Such fpotlefs Honour, fuch ingenuous Truth,
Such ripen'd Wifdom in the Bloom of Youth;
So mild, fo gentle, fo compos'd a Mind,
To fuch heroic Warmth and Courage join'd!
He too, like *Sidney*, nurs'd in Learning's Arms,
For nobler War forfook her peaceful Charms;
Like him poffefs'd of every pleafing Art,
The fecret Wifh of every Virgin's Heart;
Like him, cut off in youthful Glory's Pride,
He, unrepining, for his Country dy'd.

Here you crofs the *Serpentine* River, which brings
you into the *Elyfian* Fields.

The Shell-Bridge, by *Kent*.

The Temple of *Britifh* Worthies, by *Kent*,

a Building cut into Niches, wherein are placed the
following Buftos:

ALEXANDER POPE,

Who uniting the Correctnefs of Judgment to the Fire of Genius,
by the Melody and Power of his Numbers,
gave Sweetnefs to Senfe, and Grace to Philofophy.
He employ'd the pointed Brilliancy of Wit to chaftife the Vices,
and the Eloquence of Poetry to exalt the Virtues of human Nature;
and being without a Rival in his own Age,
imitated and tranflated, with a Spirit equal to the Originals,
the beft Poets of Antiquity.

Sir

Sir Thomas Gresham,

who by the honourable Profeſſion of a Merchant having enriched himſelf and his Country, for carrying on the Commerce of the World, built the *Royal Exchange*.

Ignatius Jones,

who to adorn his Country, introduced and rivalled the *Greek* and *Roman* Architecture.

John Milton,

whoſe ſublime and unbounded Genius equall'd a Subject that carried him beyond the Limits of the World.

William Shakespear,

whoſe excellent Genius opened to him the whole Heart of Man, all the Mines of Fancy, all the Stores of Nature; and gave him Power, beyond all other Writers, to move, aſtoniſh, and delight Mankind.

John Locke,

who, beſt of all Philoſophers, underſtood the Powers of the human Mind, the Nature, End, and Bounds of Civil Government; and with equal Courage and Sagacity, refuted the ſlaviſh Syſtems of uſurped Authority over the Rights, the Conſciences, or the Reaſon of Mankind.

Sir Isaac Newton,

whom the God of Nature made to comprehend his Works; and from ſimple Principles to diſcover the Laws never known before, and to explain the Appearances never underſtood, of this ſtupendous Univerſe.

Sir Francis Bacon, Lord Verulam,

who, by the Strength and Light of ſuperior Genius, rejecting vain Speculation and fallacious Theory, taught to purſue Truth, and improve Philoſophy by the certain Method of Experiment.

D

In

In the Niche of a Pyramid is placed a *Mercury*, with thefe Words fubfcribed:

——*Campos ducit ad Elyſios,*
——Leads to the *Elyſian* Fields.

And below this Figure is fixed a Square of black Marble with the following Lines:

Hic manus ob patriam pugnando vulnera paſſi,
Quique pii vates, & Phœbo digna locuti,
Inventas aut qui vitam excoluere per artes,
Quique ſui memores alios fecere merendo.

Here are the Bands, who for their Country bled,
And Bards, whoſe pure and ſacred Verſe is read:
Thoſe who, by Arts invented, Life improv'd,
And by their Merits, made their Mem'ries lov'd.

King A L F R E D,

the mildeft, jufteft, moft beneficent of Kings; who drove out the *Danes*, fecured the Seas, protected Learning, eftablifhed Juries, crufh'd Corruption, guarded Liberty, and was the Founder of the *Engliſh* Conftitution.

E D W A R D Prince of W A L E S,

the Terror of *Europe*, the Delight of *England*; who preferved unaltered, in the Height of Glory and Fortune, his natural Gentlenefs and Modefty.

Queen E L I Z A B E T H,

who confounded the Projects, and deftroyed the Power that threatened to opprefs the Liberties of *Europe*; fhook off the Yoke of Ecclefiaftical Tyranny; reftored Religion from the Corruptions of *Popery*; and by a wife, a moderate, and a popular Government, gave Wealth, Security, and Refpect to *England*.

King

King WILLIAM III.

who, by his Virtue and Conftancy, having faved his Country from a foreign Mafter, by a bold and generous Enterprize, preferved the Liberty and Religion of *Great-Britain*.

Sir WALTER RALEIGH,

a valiant Soldier, and an able Statefmen; who endeavouring to roufe the Spirit of his Mafter, for the Honour of his Country, againft the Ambition of *Spain*, fell a Sacrifice to the Influence of that Court, whofe Arms he had vanquifhed, and whofe Defigns he oppofed.

Sir FRANCIS DRAKE,

who, through many Perils, was the firft of *Britons* that ventured to fail round the Globe; and carried into unknown Seas and Nations the Knowledge and Glory of the *Englifh* Name.

JOHN HAMPDEN,

who, with great Spirit and confummate Abilities, began a noble Oppofition to an arbitrary Court, in Defence of the Liberties of his Country; fupported them in Parliament, and died for them in the Field.

Sir JOHN BARNARD,

who diftinguifhed himfelf in Parliament by an active and firm Oppofition to the pernicious and iniquitous Practice of Stock-jobbing: At the fame time exerting his utmoft Abilities to increafe the Strength of his Country, by reducing the Intereft of the National Debt; which he propofed to the Houfe of Commons in the Year 1737, and, with the Affiftance of Government, carried into Effect, in the Year 1750, on Terms of equal Juftice to Particulars and to the State; notwithftanding all the Impediments which private Intereft could oppofe to public Spirit.

The

The Cold Bath.

The Grotto

ſtands at the Head of the *Serpentine* River, and on each Side a Pavilion, the one ornamented with Shells, the other with Pebbles and Flints broke to Pieces. The Grotto is furniſhed with a great Number of Looking-glaſſes both on the Walls and Cieling, all in Frames of Plaiſter-work, ſet with Shells and Flints.——A Marble Statue of *Venus*, on a Pedeſtal ſtuck with the ſame.

The Temple of Concord and Victory,

is a large beautiful Building of the *Ionic* Order in the antique Taſte, and one of the principal Ornaments in the Garden.——It has ſix Statues on the Top, as big as Life, and the front Pediment is adorned with a Piece of Alt-Relief, by Mr. *Scheemaker*, repreſenting the four Quarters of the World bringing their various Products to *Britannia*.——In the Frize of the Portico is this Inſcription,

Concordiæ & Victoriæ.
To Concord and Victory.

In the Anti-Temple there are two Medallions deſcribing

Concordia Fæderatorum : Concordia Civium :
Concord of the Allies : National Concord.

Over the Door this Inſcription from *Valerius Maximus :*

Quo Tempore Salus eorum in ultimas Anguſtias deducta nullum Ambitioni Locum relinquebat.

The Times with ſuch alarming Dangers fraught,
Left not a Hope for any factious Thought.

In

In a Niche of the Temple is placed the Statue of *Libertas Publica,* Public Liberty; over which, in a Tablet from the fame Author,

.Candidis autem Animis Voluptatem præbuerint in con- fpicuo pofita quæ cuique magnifica merito contigerunt.

A fweet Senfation touches ev'ry Breaft
Of Candour's gen'rous Sentiment poffeft,
When public Services with Honour due,
Are gratefully mark'd out to public View.

On the Walls are fourteen Medallions to reprefent the taking of *Quebec, Martinico,* &c. *Louifbourg, Guadeloupe,* &c. *Montreal, Pondicherry,* &c. naval Victory off *Belleifle,* naval Victory off *Lagos, Crevelt* and *Minden, Felinghaufen, Goree* and *Senegal, Crown Point, Niagara* and *Fort du Quefne, Havannah* and *Manilla, Beau Sejour, Cherburgh* and *Belleifle*—exe- cuted from feveral of the Medals.

Here is a large and delightful Vale adorned with Statues of various Kinds, intermixed with Clumps of Trees beautifully difpofed.

From this Portico you fee in a diagonal Line, an Obelifk in the Park above an hundred Feet high, in- fcribed to Major General *Wolfe.*

Oftendunt Terris hunc tantum Fata——

The Fates but fhew him to the World.

1759.

This Obelifk ftands upon a Hill in the Approach from *Northamptonfhire,* which is very magnificent: At the Entrance there are two Lodges, from whence a very broad and long Line conducting you through Woods, is terminated by the Temple of Concord and Victory.—In the other diagonal Line from the Temple,

Temple, ſtands a lofty fluted Column erected to the Memory of the late Lord Viſcount *Cobham*.

A Gravel Path now leads by the Statue of *Hercules* and *Antæus*, ſkirting the Valley, to the Circle of the dancing Faun, ſurrounded with the Statues of Shepherds and Shepherdeſſes.

      " And every Shepherd tells his Tale
      " Under a Hawthorn in the Dale."

Winding through a Wood, not far diſtant, riſe

The Fane and Statue of Paſtoral Poetry,

Holding in her Hand a Scroll with theſe Words,

      Paſtorum Carmina Canto.

      I tune the Shepherd's Lay.

The Fane is adorned with Terms, *&c.* Here a moſt pleaſing Foreſt-ſcene preſents itſelf, formed by extenſive Lawns of the Park, bounded with old Oaks : You next croſs over the Valley and ſoon come to

      Lord *Cobham*'s Pillar.

Round the Baſe of the Column is written

Ut L. Luculli ſummi Viri Virtutem quis? At quam multi Villarum Magnificentiam imitati ſunt?

As in the Inſtance of *L. Lucullus*, a truly great Man! who hath imitated his Virtues? But how many his Example, in magnificently adorning their Country-ſeats?

                          On

On the Pedeſtal are the following Inſcriptions :

On one Side,

To preſerve the Memory of her Huſband,

Anne Viſcounteſs *Cobham*

Cauſed this Pillar to be erected

In the Year 1747.

On the oppoſite Side,

Quatenus nobis denegatur diu vivere,

relinquamus aliquid,

quo nos vixiſſe teſtemur.

Inaſmuch as the Portion of Life allotted to us is ſhort,

let us leave ſomething behind us,

to ſhew that we have lived.

The Lady's Temple,

is built upon Groin Arches, with *Venetian* Windows ;
a neat Stair-caſe leads you up to a Hall, the Walls of
which are adorned with the following Paintings by
Mr. *Sleter.*

On the Right-hand are Ladies, employing themſelves in Needle and Shell-work.—On the oppoſite
Side, are Ladies diverting themſelves with Painting
and Muſic.

The *Gothic* Temple,

is a large Building of red Stone, 70 Feet high, upon
a riſing Ground, adorned in the *Gothic* Way with
carved Work and painted Glaſs. The Diſpoſition
within is very beautiful. You enter a circular Room,
the

the Dome of which is ornamented with the Defcents of the *Temple* Family. On the fecond Story, is a Gallery : The Tower affords a very extenfive View round the Country.

The Hill round the Temple is adorned with very good Statues, by *Ryfbrack*, of the feven *Saxon* Deities, who gave Names to the Days of the Week.—The Portico of the Temple of *Concord* and *Victory* has a beautiful Effect from this Place.

The *Palladian* Bridge,

The Roof of which is fupported by *Ionic* Pillars.

From hence you pafs into the great Terras-walk, which is 3000 Feet long.

The Temple of Friendfhip,

is a large Structure of the *Doric* Order. On the Outfide is this Motto :

Amicitiæ S.————Sacred to Friendfhip.

The Infide is furnifhed with the Bufts of the late Vifcount *Cobham* and his Friends, *viz. Frederick* Prince of *Wales* ; the Earls of *Chefterfield, Weftmore-land*, and *Marchmont* ; the Lords *Cobham, Gower*, and *Bathurft* ; *Richard Grenville*, now Earl *Temple* ; *William Pitt*, now Earl of *Chatham* ; and *George Lyttleton*, now Lord *Lyttleton.*

The Roof is painted emblematically, and ornamented in a very gay Manner.

The Pebble Alcove,

is a little Grot neatly adorned with Pebbles ; his Lordfhip's Arms are curioufly wrought upon the back Wall with the fame Materials.

CONGREVE's Monument, by *Kent.*

The Embellifhments round it are defigned to exprefs the Poet's Genius in the dramatic Way ; upon
the

the Top fits a Monkey viewing himfelf in a Mirror, with this Infcription :

Vitæ imitatio,
Confuetudinis fpeculum,
Comædia.

Comedy is the Imitation of Life, and the Mirror of Fafhion.

The Poet's Effigies lies in a carelefs Pofture on one Side, and on the other is placed this Epitaph :

Ingenio
Acri, faceto, expolito,
Moribufque
Urbanis, candidis, facillimis,
GULIELMI CONGREVE,
Hoc
Qualecunque defiderii fui
Solamen fimul ac
Monumentum
Pofuit COBHAM.
1736.

To the fprightly, entertaining, elegant
Wit,
and the polifhed, candid, eafy
Manners
Of WILLIAM CONGREVE,
This
in fome Sort a Confolation ;
and a Memorial of his affectionate Regret,
was erected by
COBHAM.

N. B. The Gardens contain between three and four hundred Acres.

E   EXPLANA

EXPLANATION *of the* PLANS,

A The principal Floor of Stowe-House.
a The State Bed-Chamber.
b The State Dressing-Room.
c The State Gallery.
d The Corridore.
e The Servants Bed-Chamber.
f An open Gallery.
g The Drawing Room.
h The Stucco Gallery.
i The Dining-Room.
k The Bed Chamber, and Dressing-Room.
l The Hall.
m A Dressing-Room.
n A Bed-Chamber.
o The great Stair-Case.
p The Corridore.
q The Gallery.
r The Grenville Room.
s The Dressing Room.
t The Bed Chamber.
v An open Gallery, and Chinese Closet.
w A Bed-Chamber.
x The Chapel.
Fig. 1. The Temple of Concord, and Victory.
Fig. 2. The Gothic Temple.

Fig. 3. The Lady's Temple.
Fig. 4. The Temple of Friendship.
Fig. 5. The Temple of Antient Virtue
Fig. 6. The Temple of Venus.
Fig. 7. The Rotundo.
Fig. 8. The Temple of Bacchus.
Fig. 9. The Fane of Pastoral Poetry.
Fig. 10. The Egyptian Pyramid.
Fig. 11. One of the Pavilions at the Entrance to the Garden.
Fig. 12. One of the Pavilions at the Entrance to the Park.
Fig. 13. Dido's Cave.
Fig. 14. The Temple of British Worthies.
Fig. 15. The Hermitage.
Fig. 16. Nelson's Seat.
Fig. 17. The Grotto.
Fig. 18. The Cold Bath.
Fig. 19. The Palladian Bridge.
Fig. 20. The Shell Bridge, by the same Scale.
Fig. 21. The New Bridge, leading to the Lodges.

Note, Where there is but one Scale in a Plate, it is applicable to all the Plans in that Plate.

The Scales are of Feet.

A

DESCRIPTION

OF · THE

H O U S E.

B Y a noble Flight of Steps defigned by Signior *Borra*, ornamented with Stone Balluftrades, you afcend to a grand Apartment, called

The Saloon,

43 Feet by 22 Feet.

It is hung with fine Tapeftry reprefenting the Functions of the Cavalry, with Crimfon Cafoy Chairs and Settees.

The Paintings are,

1. A Landfchape.
2. A Flower Piece.
3. A Fruit Piece.
4. A Portrait of Lord *Chatham* over the Chimney.

E 2   5. A

5. A Portrait of Lady *Chatham* at the other End.
Two Marble Bufts, one at each End.

The Hall.

36 Feet by 22 Feet 9 Inches; defigned and painted
by *Kent.*

The Cieling is finely adorned with the Signs of the
Zodiack.
Over the Chimney, is a very curious Piece of Alt-
Relief : The Story is *Darius*'s Tent.
Eleven Marble Bufts.
The Walls are adorned with Ornaments of Fef-
toons, &c.
Two Marble Tables.
A large white Marble Slab.
A Marble Ciftern.

A Bed-Chamber, and two Dreffing-Rooms hung with yellow Damafk.

A curious Cheft inlaid with Mother of Pearl.
An old Japan Cabinet, with ornamental China
upon it.
Glaffes over the Chimnies.

A Dreffing-Room.

Prince *Henry* at full Length over the Chimney.
A fine Cabinet, with old China Jars upon it.

A Bed-Chamber,

with rich crimfon Cafoy Bed and Furniture.
A Portrait of a late Countefs of *Dorfet* at full
Length, over the Chimney.

A Dreffing-

A Dreffing-Room.

A Piece of ftill Life over the Chimney.

The grand Stair-Cafe,

ornamented with Iron Work.

Three Cieling-Pieces, painted by *Sclater*, *viz.*
1. Juftice and Peace.
2. Fame and Victory.
3. Plenty and Conftancy.

The Walls are adorned with warlike Pieces.

The Stone Stair-Cafe,

with Iron Ballufters, the Walls ornamented with Medallions.————Leading into a private Apartment below Stairs,

A Billiard-Room.
A Parlour.
A Breakfafting-Room, and
A Waiting-Room.

Second and third Pair of Stairs, a Number of Bed-Chambers, and two Dreffing-Rooms to each Bed-Chamber.

The Chapel,

37 Feet by 20 Feet 10 Inches, and 26 Feet high, wainfcotted with Cedar, with a Gallery of the fame, hung with crimfon Velvet, under which are Seats for the Servants.

Over the Communion-Table is a fine Painting of the Refurrection, by *Tintoretto*, and over that is the King's Arms finely carved and ornamented.

Above the Cedar Wainfcot, are the following Paintings at full Length:

Mofes and *Aaron.*

Two of the Apoftles, St. *Peter* and St. *Paul.*
The four Evangelifts.

There are three other Paintings, *viz.*

1. The Afcenfion.
2. The Baptifm.
3. The Salutation of the Virgin *Mary.*

The Cieling is the fame as at the Chapel Royal at St. *James's,* and the Cedar Wainfcot enriched with elegant Carvings, by *Gybbons.*

Her Ladyfhip's Dreffing-Room,

with Hangings, Chairs, and Window-Curtains of fine printed Cotton.

A fine old Japan Cabinet, ornamented with China Jars.

A fine View of *Pekin,* over the Chimney-Piece, by *Jolli.*

The Bed-Chamber,

with Hangings, Chairs, and Window-Curtains of the fame.

A Picture of a *Chinefe* Temple over the Chimney, by *Jolli.*

The Chinefe Clofet,

Or a Repofitory of her Ladyfhip's valuable China.

The Japan and Ornaments were a Prefent of the late Prince and Princefs of *Wales.*——From this Clofet you enter a Colonade, ornamented with Paintings, by *Sclater.*

It is likewife curioufly embellifhed with Exoticks and Flowering Shrubs.

The

The GRENVILLE Room,

29 Feet 8 Inches by 26 Feet 3 Inches, and 19 Feet 4 Inches high,

hung with green Velvet, and ornamented with the following Portraits, all at full Length, except the firſt:

Over the Chimney.

1. The late Counteſs *Temple*, Mother to the preſent Earl.
2. The Right Honourable *George Grenville*, late Firſt Lord of the Treaſury, and Chancellor of the *Exchequer*.
3. The Right Honourable *James Grenville*, Vice Treaſurer of *Ireland*, and one of his Majeſty's moſt honourable Privy Council.
4. His Excellency *Henry Grenville*, Ambaſſador to the *Ottoman Porte*.
5. The Honourable *Thomas Grenville*, who was killed in the Defence of his Country, on board the *Defiance*, of which he was Captain.
6. Lady *Cobham*.
7. Sir *Thomas Temple*.
8. Lady *Heſter Temple*, who lived to ſee 700 deſcended from her own Body. Vide *Fuller*'s *Worthies*.

Three Book-Caſes.

A Dining-Room,

Ornamented with twelve Marble Buſts of the *Roman* Emperors and Empreſſes.

The Paintings are,

1. The preſent Earl *Temple*, by *Ramſey*.

2. The

2. The prefent Countefs *Temple*, by *Hoare*, both at full Length.

3. A Picture, by *Pinani*, over the Chimney.

The following Marble Statues of

1. *Venus* and *Adonis*, by *Scheemaker*.
2. *Vertumnus* and *Pomona*, by *Delvot*.
3. A *Narciffus*.
Two Tables of Oriental Alabafter.
Two Marble Cifterns.

A Drawing-Room,

hung with three fine Pieces of Tapeftry, as follows:

1. A *Dutch* Fifhery, from *Teniers*.
2. A *Dutch* Wake, from *Teniers*.
3. A beautiful Reprefentation of a Farm.
Gobeline Tapeftry Chairs.
A Picture, by *Pinani*, over the Chimney.
Two Tables of Marble of *Sienna*.
Two Pier Glaffes.
Two Bufts, one over each Door.

A Waiting-Room.

The Paintings are,

1. *Joan* of *Arc* over the Chimney, by *Albert Durer*.
2. *Cymon* and *Iphigenia*.
3. *Orodes* ordering melted Gold to be poured into the Mouth of *Craffus*.
4. Two Landfchapes, by *Salvator Rofa*.
5. A Head, by *Cornelius Johnfon*.
6. Two Landfchapes, one over each Door.

A Pri-

A Private Breakfasting-Room.

The Paintings are,

1. A Portrait of Colonel *Stanyan*, by *Dobfon*.
2. The Reprefentation of the Holy Lamb, by *Rubens*.
3. Four Landfchapes, by *Pouffin*.
4. Two Ditto, by *Coten*.
5. A large Picture of young *Bacchanals*.
Two Pier-glaffes.
A Tortoife-fhell Commode.

A Drawing-Room,

hung with yellow Silk Damafk, trimm'd with Silver Lace, Chairs and Window-curtains the fame.

The Paintings are,

1. Over the Chimney, a Picture of *Samfon* in the Prifon at *Gaza*, by *Rembrandt*.—The King of *Pruffia* has one of the fame in his Collection.
2. Two Saints, a St. *Laurence* and St. *Stephen*, one over each Door.
3. Two large Landfchapes, by *Horizonti*.
4. *Mofes* burying the *Egyptian*, by *Pcu ffin*.
5. A Sea-port, by a *Flemifh* Mafter.
6. A Landfchape with dancing Satyrs, by *Paul Brill*.
7. A Landfchape, by *Claude Lorain*.
8. A fmall Landfchape of *Acis* and *Galatea*, by *Millè*.
A curious inlaid Cabinet, with Chimney and Pier-glafs in gilt Frames.

A Private Dining-Room,

blue Silk Damafk Furniture, with Chimney and Pier-glaffes.

F   The

The Paintings are,

1. A Portrait of *Rubens*'s Wife, by *Rubens*.
2. A Knight of the *Bath*, by *Vandyke*.
3. The Rape of *Helen*, by *Thefeus*. ⎫ Both by
4. The Return of *Chryfeïs* to her Father. ⎭ *Primaticio*.
5. The Duke of *Sully*, or Marquis *de Veuville*, by *Vandyke*.
6. The Dutchefs of *Richmond*, by Sir *Peter Lely*.
7. The Marriage of *Cana*, by *Baffan*.
8. Two Pieces of Ruins, by *Canaletti*.
9. *Vulcan* and *Venus*, by *Primaticio*.

A Waiting-Room,

hung with yellow Silk Damafk, trimm'd with Silver Lace.

The Paintings are,

1. A Portrait of *Oliver Cromwell*, by old *Richardfon*.
2. A Dancing at the Marriage of the Duke of *Mantua*, by *Tintoretto*.
3. *Samfon* and *Dalilah*, by *Guercino*.
4. A *Silenus*, by *Rubens*.
5. A Landfchape, with Figures and Cattle, by *Baffan*.
6. A Piece of Ruins, by *Viviano*.
A Chimney-glafs.

The State Apartment.

1. The State Gallery,

70 Feet 9 Inches by 25 Feet,——and 22 Feet high.
Two Marble Chimney-pieces of *Sienna*, &c. by Mr. *Lovel*.
The Cieling finely ornamented with Paintings and Gilding, by *Sclater*.

Two

Two fine Marble Tables of *Nero Antico*, with two large Pier-glasses.

The Walls are adorned with curious Pieces of Tapeftry, *viz.*

1. The Triumph of *Ceres.*
2. The Triumph of *Bacchus.*
3. The Triumph of *Venus.*
4. The Triumph of *Mars.*
5. The Triumph of *Diana.*

The Piers adorned with Trophies.

Two Chimnies, the upper Part of which are adorned with Gilding and Carving.

1. A Goddefs conducting Learning to Truth.
2. Reprefenting *Mercury* conducting tragic and comic Poetry to the Hill of *Parnaffus.*

Four emblematical Paintings in Clare-Obfcure.

The Chairs, Settees, and Window-curtains of blue Silk Damafk.

2. The State Dreffing-Room,

24 Feet 8 Inches by 30 Feet—and 19 Feet 4 Inches high, hung with blue Damafk, Chairs and Window-curtains of the fame.

The Doors and Cieling are finely ornamented with Carving and Gilding.

The Chimney-piece, by Mr. *Lovel.*

The Paintings are,

A fine Portrait of the late Lord *Cobham*, by Sir *Godfrey Kneller.*

Four Converfation Pieces, by *Francefco Cippo.*

Venus binding the Eyes of a Cupid, and the Graces offering Tribute, by *Titian.*

Two fine whole Lengths of King *George* III. and Queen *Charlotte*, by *Ramfay.*

A Marble Table, with a fine Pier-glafs.

3. The State Bed-Chamber,

50 Feet 8 Inches, by 25 Feet 10 Inches——and 18 Feet 8 Inches high.

The Bed and Cieling, by Signior *Borra*.——The Chairs and Hangings of Crimſon Damaſk.——The Pillars of the *Corinthian* Order, the whole finely carved and gilt.

A *Madona* from the School of *Rubens*.

A large Glaſs over the Chimney.

A very curious Chimney-piece of white Marble, deſigned by Signior *Borra*, and executed by Mr. *Lovel*.

Two Cupids, with Branches for Candles in their Hands, by Mr. *Lovel*.

Two Marble Tables of *Giallo Antico*.

Two fine large Pier-glaſſes.

The Cieling ornamented with the Inſignia of the Garter.

4. The State Cloſet,

hung with Crimſon Damaſk, finely ornamented with Carving and Gilding.——Out of which you go into a Colonade, where you have a beautiful View of the Gardens and Country.

A Paſſage,

ornamented with Marble Buſts.

A Grand Stair-Caſe,

adorned with Paintings of the Four Seaſons.

The Cieling repreſents the Riſing Sun, by *Phœbus* in his Car.

The whole Length of the Houſe, including the Offices, is 900 Feet.

F I N I S.

.